PIANO • VOCAL • GUITAR

BRAINWASHED

by George Harrison

Art direction by thenewno2. © Umlaut Corporation

ISBN 978-0-634-05777-9

HAL•LEONARD®
CORPORATION

7777 W. BLUEMOUND RD. P.O. BOX 13819 MILWAUKEE, WI 53213

Visit Hal Leonard Online at
www.halleonard.com

CONTENTS

ANY ROAD

Words and Music by
GEORGE HARRISON

6

oh, Lord, ___ we pay the price ___ with the spin of the wheel, ___ with the

roll of the dice. Ah yeah, ___ you pay your fare, ___ and if you

don't know where you're ___ go - ing, ___ an - y road will take ___ you there. ___

D.S. al Coda

P2 VATICAN BLUES
(Last Saturday Night)

Words and Music by
GEORGE HARRISON

Moderate Blues

PISCES FISH

Words and Music by
GEORGE HARRISON

22

LOOKING FOR MY LIFE

Words and Music by
GEORGE HARRISON

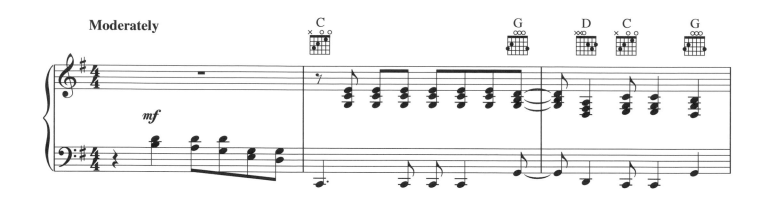

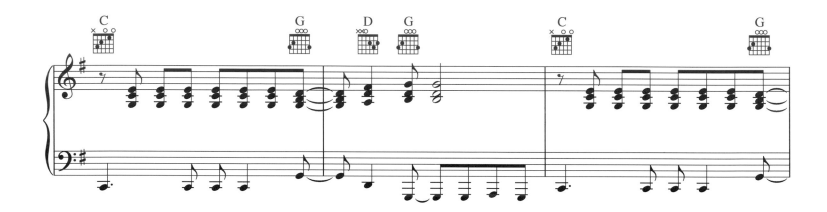

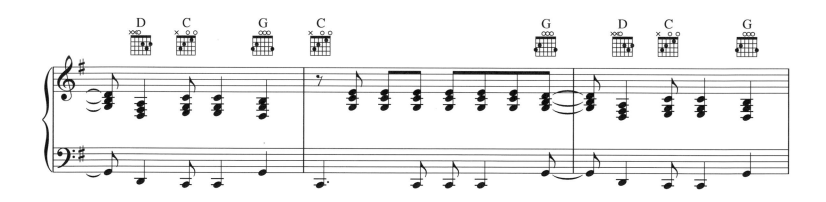

28

RISING SUN

Words and Music by
GEORGE HARRISON

38

MARWA BLUES

Words and Music by
GEORGE HARRISON

STUCK INSIDE A CLOUD

Words and Music by
GEORGE HARRISON

Never slept so little.
I made some ex-hi-bi-tion.

Never smoked so much.
I lost my will to eat.

Lost my con-cen-
On-ly thing that

tra-tion, I could e-ven lose my touch.
mat-ters to me is to touch your lo-tus feet.

44

RUN SO FAR

Words and Music by
GEORGE HARRISON

50

NEVER GET OVER YOU

Words and Music by
GEORGE HARRISON

BETWEEN THE DEVIL AND THE DEEP BLUE SEA

Lyric by TED KOEHLER
Music by HAROLD ARLEN

60

ROCKING CHAIR IN HAWAII

Words and Music by
GEORGE HARRISON

Moderate Blues

I'm go - ing down to the __ riv - er, __ gon - na take __
don't get the __ pic - ture, __ you

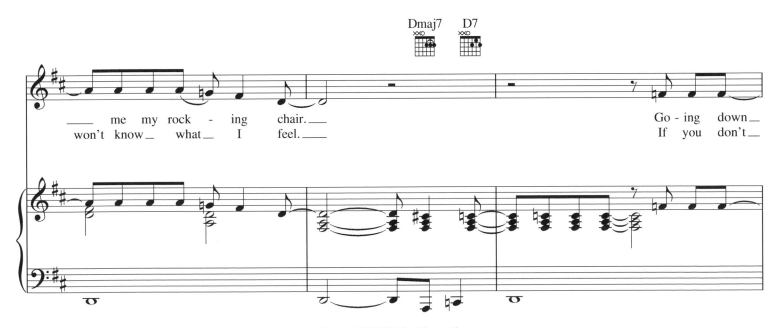

__ me my rock - ing chair. __ Go - ing down __
won't know __ what __ I feel. __ If you don't __

BRAINWASHED

Words and Music by
GEORGE HARRISON

Brain - washed in our child - hood,___
Brain - washed by the Nik - kei.___ I'm brain -

_out the spir - i - tual light.___
ist - ence, knowl - edge,_ bliss.___
_ ac - cept _ de - feat.___

1. *Instrumental*
2. *(Spoken:)* *The soul does not love.* *It is love itself.*

It does not exist. *It is existence itself.*

C/E D5 5fr A5 5fr C G5 3fr F
- thing I for - got, (God, God, God,) down on
C A5 5fr C G5 3fr F
Bull - shit Av - e - nue. (God, God, God,) if we can on -
C/E D5 5fr A5 5fr C G5 3fr F
- ly stop the rot. (God, God, God,) wish that
G5 3fr G7 G6
You'd brain - wash us, too.

Na - mah Par - var - ti Pa - ta - ye_____ Ha - re Ha - re.

Shi - va Shi - va Shan - kar - a Ma - ha - de - va._____

Ha - re Ha - re Ha - re Ha - re Ma - ha - de - va._____

Shi - va Shi - va Shan - kar - a Ma - ha - de - va._____

78